WEST CHAR

D0687141

MAY 27 2006

LAS VEGAS-CLARK COUNTY
LIBRARY DISTRICT
833 LAS VEGAS BLVD, N.
LAS VEGAS, NEVADA 89101

Making Music

Shaking

Angela Aylmore

Raintree

Chicago, Illinois

© 2006 Raintree
Published by Raintree, a division of Reed Elsevier, Inc.
Chicago, Illinois
Customer Service 888-363-4266
Visit our website at www.raintreelibrary.com

All rights reserved. No part of this book may be reproduced or transmitted in any form or by any means, electronic or mechanical, including photocopying, recording, taping, or any information storage or retrieval system, without permission in writing from the publisher.
For information, address the publisher:
Raintree, 100 N. LaSalle, Suite 1200, Chicago, IL 60602

Printed and bound by South China Printing Company.
10 09 08 07 06
10 9 8 7 6 5 4 3 2 1

Library of Congress Cataloging-in-Publication Data:

Aylmore, Angela.
  Shaking / Angela Aylmore.
      p. cm. -- (Making music)
  Includes index.
  ISBN 1-4109-1607-3 (library binding-hardcover) -- ISBN 1-4109-1612-X
(pbk.) 1. Percussion instruments--Juvenile literature. I. Title. II. Series:
Aylmore, Angela. Making music.
  ML1030.A97 2005
  786.8'19--dc22
                         2005002516

Acknowledgments
The publishers would like to thank the following for permission to reproduce photographs:
Alamy pp. **8**, **16**, **18**; Corbis pp. **5a** (David Katzenstein), **13**; Getty Image p. **9** (Photodisc); Harcourt Education pp. **4a** (Gareth Boden), **4b**, **5b**, **6**, **7**, **10a**, **10b**, **11**, **12**, **14**, **15**, **17**, **19**, **20**, **21**, **22-23** (Tudor Photography).

Cover photograph of a boy shaking a rattle, reproduced with permission of Harcourt Education/Tudor Photography.

Every effort has been made to contact copyright holders of any material reproduced in this book. Any omissions will be rectified in subsequent printings if notice is given to the publishers.

> Some words are shown in bold, **like this**. You can find out what they mean by looking in the glossary on page 24.

Contents

Let's Make Music!

We can make **music** by **shaking**!

Ben shakes his tambourine.

Ding!

Ring the bells!

Play the maracas.

Cha-cha, cha-cha

Pitter-patter goes the rainmaker.

Play the Tambourine

Can you play the tambourine?

Shake it gently. Keep it soft.

tr-tr-tr-tr

tr–tr–tr–tr

Shake it hard.
Make it loud.

Ding, Dong Bells

Can you play the bells?

A small bell plays
a high **note**.

A big bell
plays a
low note.

Make Your Own

Can you make a shaker?

Look at my shaker.

Look at my shaker.

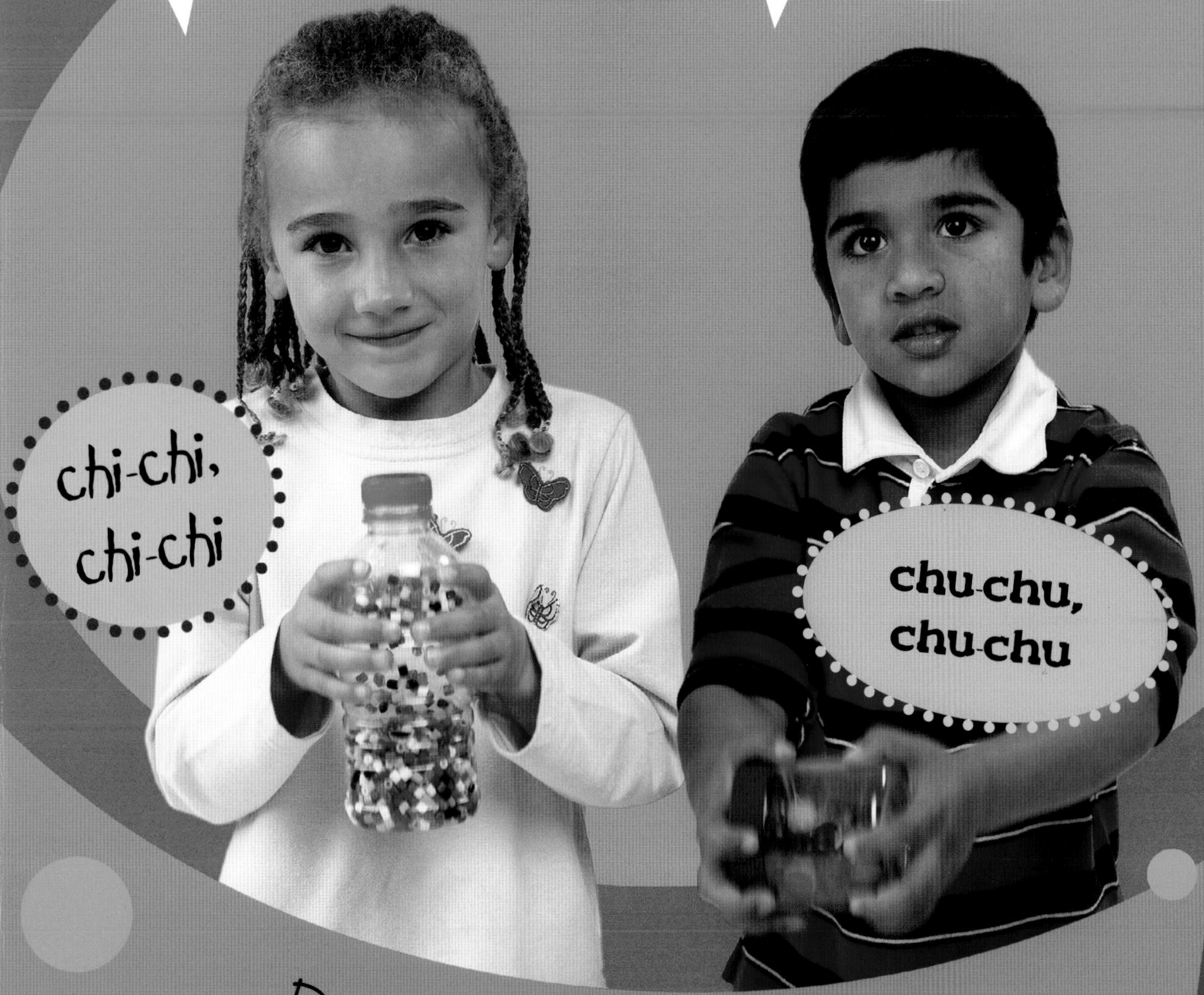

Do they sound the same?

Sounds Like...

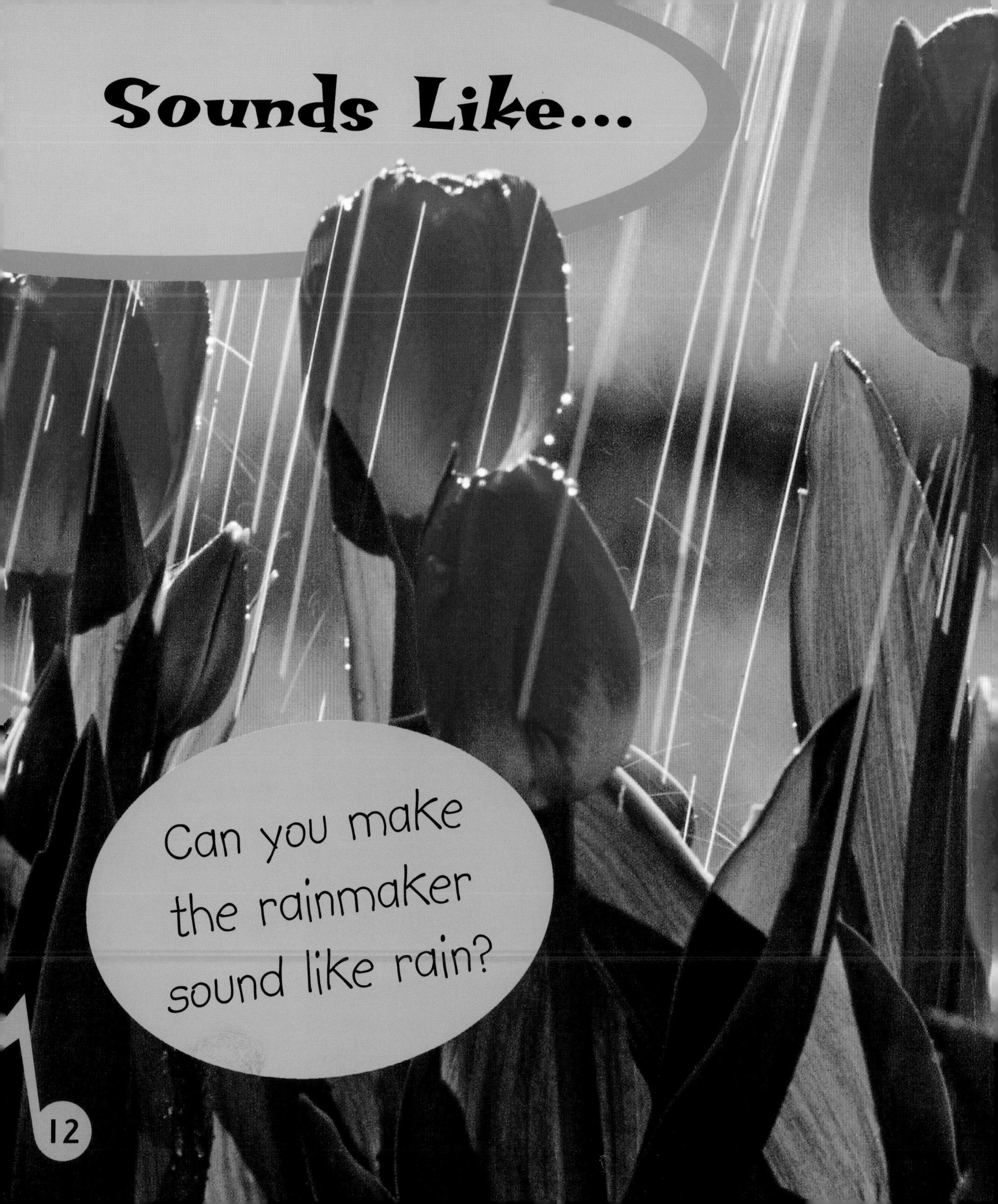

Can you make the rainmaker sound like rain?

pitter, patter

pitter, patter

Music For a Story

Let's use **music** to tell a story!

The itsy bitsy spider climbed up the waterspout.

Down came the rain and washed the spider out.

Woosh!

15

What Is It?

This is a sistrum. It comes from Egypt. It sounds like a rattle.

Can you play a rattle?
Shake it slowly.
Shake it quickly.

Use Your Body

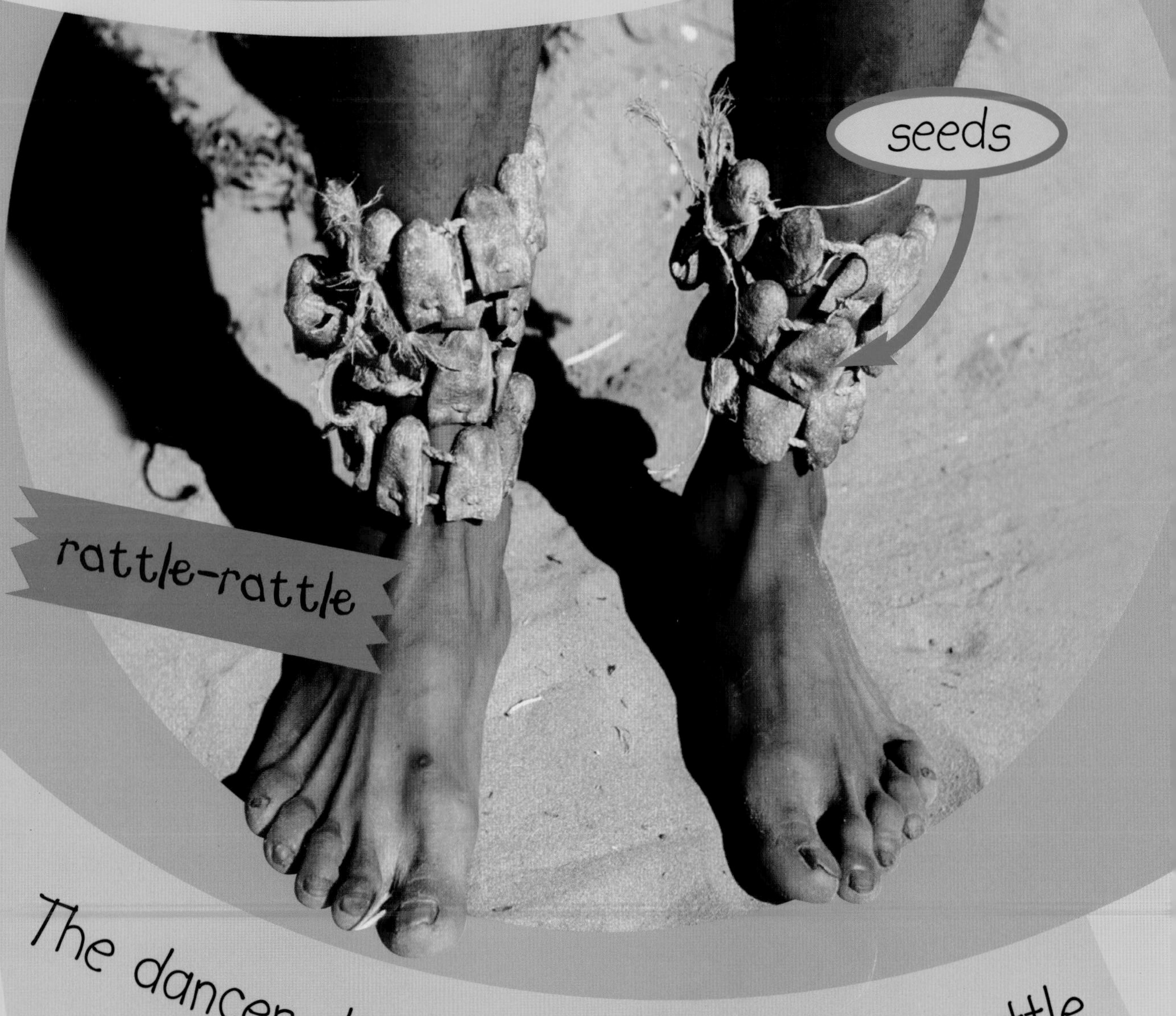

seeds

rattle-rattle

The dancer dances. The seeds rattle-rattle.

Can you **shake** your body and make the bells ring?

jingle-jangle
jingle-jangle

Listen Carefully

What can you hear?
What makes that sound?

ch ch

maracas

violin

triangle

recorder

It's the maracas!

21

All Together Now!

Glossary

music a mixture of sounds to express an idea or emotion
note a specific single sound, which can be written
shake to move something from side to side

Index

Notes for Adults

Making Music provides children with an opportunity to think about sound and the different ways instruments can be played to create music. The concept of volume, rhythm, speed, and pitch are introduced, and children are encouraged to think about how controlling their movements can create different sounds when they play instruments.

This book looks at ways of creating music by shaking. It introduces different instruments that are shaken and the sounds they make. Comparisons are made between high and low, loud and quiet, fast and slow sounds.

Follow-up activities

• With their eyes closed, ask the children to identify the different instruments that you play.

• Can the children use their instruments to create sound effects for different stories or nursery rhymes?

• See if the children can come up with sounds to represent different types of weather, such as rain, wind, sunshine, or a storm.